I0697389

RICH IN
MIND,
RICH
IN
POCKET
A Complete
Accelerator
guide on how to
discover your
business, start
it and close
sales crazily.
DR ANNASTASIA NZE

RICH IN MIND, RICH IN POCKET

A complete Accelerator guide on how to discover your business, start it and close sales crazily.

Dr. Annastasia Nze

You can start from where you are right now to a level where nothing else can stop you.

Annastasia

I believe in unlocking potentials! I believe in becoming! there's no height you can't attain if you believe and invest in yourself

Annastasia.

TABLE OF CONTENTS

INTRODUCTION

This few paged book contains in it everything you need to know on how to make it big not just in business but life in it's entirety.

I poured out my heart in this book because I know it'll pass a message to anyone reading it.

Digest every part of this book.

Do not skip anything. If the techniques written in this book don't work for you, kindly ask for a refund.

Your friend, Annastasia.

Chapter 1

Who is Annastasia and why should you listen to me?

I am Nze Annastasia Chikodi, a medical doctor and a digital marketing expert.
I am popularly known as d_affiliate doc on Twitter.
I am currently doing my housemanship in one of the teaching hospitals in Nigeria.
You are probably wondering how I'm combining the both. Don't worry, in the course of reading this book you'd know.

My journey as a digital marketer has been an amazing one. I major on Affiliate marketing but this book goes beyond Affiliate marketing.
It talks about how to start your online business and how to sell anything to anybody crazily.

I have trained and still train hundreds of people on the online space and I'm proud to say that they are doing amazingly well. Most of them are earning in 7 figures.

I'm not from a rich background so I know what it means to be in lack. I was once there. It isn't an awesome experience but trust me, you are not disadvantaged if that is your case. I'll tell you why. As at this time last year, I was a broke final year Medical student. It was too bad that I started searching for what to do online.
Heard about Affiliate marketing before but I didn't know what it was all about.
I started making research on it.
That was how I got to find out about various Affiliate marketing platforms like clickbank, herculist Tapestri etc but I was still confused. Remember, I was still broke.
Having done some online businesses in the past like network marketing, I just needed the one that will stand the test of time for me.

So one of those days I was scrolling through LinkedIn when I came across an online opportunity on Affiliate marketing.
I connected with the poster (now my mentor) who explained what it was all about to me. I knew it was for me but money for registration was war.

I learnt about leveraging on good debts which I'll
discuss in the later pages of this book and adopted
it.
That was it. I didn't let my empty pocket limit me.
I started my online business and a few months
down the line, my life has changed for good; from
mindset to high income skills to sales expertise to
making money and traveling around the world.
This massive knowledge that I've gained is what
I'm going to share with you in this book.
I will take you from where you are right now to
earning 5 to 7 figures online. You are in for a big
thing.

So continue reading and you'll find value as you
progress.

Chapter 2

The Winner's mindset.

Who is a winner? A winner isn't necessarily someone who has passed an exam or someone who has won a lottery.
A winner for me is a risk taker. Someone who must have failed multiple times and yet didn't quit. Someone who is willing to challenge himself in order to break new grounds! Someone with an abundance mindset.

What does it mean for a man to possess the mindset of a winner?
Let's take it from the scratch: there are two types of mindset; the first one is the Prosperity/abundance/winner's mindset.
The second is the poor/poverty mindset.
An abundance mindset says I don't have it yet but I'll have it. I'm not there yet but I'll get there.
Poverty mindset is a killer of destinies! Poverty mindset will rip you off everything you are meant to become or have in this life and leave you with

nothing. Poverty mindset says I'm not worthy of the good things of life. I don't deserve the best.

This is not meant for me. Poverty mindset gets angry with other people when they're winning. It doesn't look for how to be better in order to win . Poverty mindset is blaming everyone for not having money (parents, siblings, friends, and relatives).
Poverty mindset says that those that are getting results online are better than him. Poverty mindset is a disease, a very deadly one.

Abundance mindset says I'll succeed in this business or career no matter the challenges life throws at me. Abundance mindset doesn't get offended when people are winning, it claps for them knowing that they will be celebrated one day. Abundance mindset isn't jealousy! Abundance mindset is already wealthy in mind but keeps looking for the best ways to make it a reality.
I adopted this and I have become it.
I affirm to myself everyday declaring all I want and all I am and I see it happening in my life. It might not be all evident in my life right now but give it time.
When I started my online business, people kept asking how much I had made. That if I show them

how much I've made that they'll start theirs. My only response was, "I haven't started earning yet but give it time ".

Few months down the line, I've made 7 figures in this business. I'm traveling around the world and I'm coaching hundreds of people who are already course and book creators earning hugely on the online space. You see that? You are the only rain maker of your destiny. No one else will decide what your destiny will be for you; you are the only one that will do that. This is why you should develop and train your mind with the right things. This is why you should drop that poverty mindset and adopt an abundance mindset.

  I want you to see yourself as a millionaire! I want you to see you being celebrated! I want you to see yourself touching thousands of lives on the online space; even offline. I want you to see people drawing to the light you carry. Can you envision that? That is who you are meant to be ; a champion. Now there's work to do.
If you must be a winner, then you should know the three core enemies of man: Fear, Laziness and procrastination.

The fear of the unknown, uncertainties, what will people say? Will they listen to me? Will they buy from me? What if I don't succeed? These are the questions going through your mind right now.
See champ; FEAR is a False Evidence Appearing Real ----- *Nick Vujicic.*
Expectations of a false outcome which we imagine so vividly that it appears real in our minds -so real that even our body reacts like it is already happening now. This is why you don't even realize on time that FEAR is your enemy.
It will deprive you of all the good things you deserve in life.

The second one is **laziness**. This is idleness. Some people can lie on the bed pressing their phone all day long. They just do not feel like doing anything but feel that they deserve everything. Laziness is your greatest enemy.

A price must be paid! Yes! A price must be paid for a life to be changed! For everyone one you see enjoying today, a price has been paid; either their grandparents or their parents or them. A price must be paid. So do not feel bad if your parents didn't pay that price of giving you a golden spoon kind of life; it is your turn now to work so your children will not suffer too. So conquer laziness today.

The third core enemy of man is **Procrastination**. This one presents itself as your friend but trust me, it is your worst enemy.
I'll do it later! I'll do it tomorrow! I'll do it next week! I'll do it next month! Okay, next year! You see that? You might even find a cogent reason why you're not doing it; a very valid and justifiable reason why you keep carrying it over. This is why I stated that it presents itself as your friend but kills you gradually.

Now until you overcome these three, you wouldn't win big on the online space. You need to conquer them today.
Let's move on champ.

Chapter 3

What most people don't know!

Aaah! Anna, are you serious? You mean that this business you started has taken you to Dubai?
Anna, do you mean that you earned this in a week online? Do you mean that you sell something to people you don't know? How? This is what most people don't know. They don't even know that this phone in their hands can change their lives. The world has gone digitized and people are making it big online.
Gone are the days when you can sell only if you have a physical shop. This is the 21st century and you should evolve as others are evolving.
You can sell online and the strategy is simple. I'll talk about it soon.

Chapter 4

What is in your hands? Think it!

This chapter might be the chapter you have been searching all your life.
Let's get to work. *Deuteronomy 28:12:* The Lord shall open unto thee His good treasure, the heaven to give the rain unto thy land in His season , and TO BLESS THE WORK OF THINE HAND: and thou shalt lend unto many nations and thou shall not borrow.

Exodus 4:2 (KJV): And the Lord said to Him, "What is that in your hand?" He said , "A rod".
You see? Throughout the bible, God always had an interest in whatever is in a person's possession.

Now take a look at this; God is a respecter of principles. He detests laziness.
You cannot just be doing nothing and expect God to bless you. What is He blessing? He said He'll bless the work of your hands meaning that He

cannot bless an empty hand. You can't get lucky once or twice but a valuable person would always attract favour continuously because there's something in his hands. Do you understand?

Now the question is, **"WHAT IS IN YOUR HANDS?"** Can you pause and give it a thought? Now let me make it easy for you; what is that thing you have passion for? What is that thing you're good at? What is that thing you enjoy doing? If you can't answer these questions, this means that you have to find something right away. You should because time and tide wait no man.

One more thing; that I said you should think about what you have passion for doesn't mean that everything you think of would sell online.

Firstly, you should ask yourself; is this what people want?
You should have a hungry market! It should be what people are looking for. Not what you think they'll need.

Let me tell you a story:

I bought a piggy box (kolo) in my 4th year in the
university and saved 21k from July to December.
I was so amazed because it was just my small
changes that I was inserting inside the box.
So during resumption in January of the following
year, I just reluctantly posted on my status that
people should buy piggy boxes while coming back
to school in order to save. I told them on my status
how I was able to save last year with my piggy box.

That was many people started chatting up; "Anna,
where can I get it?" I got this particular reply from
20 persons. So what I did was to use the money my
allowance then to get 20 piggy banks and chatted
those people up that I had gotten it for them. I sold
it at affordable prices and that was how I ended up
selling more than 120 piggy banks that year.i was
fondly called "Anna piggy banks" then...lol.

You see? My market was already waiting for me.
They wanted piggy banks and I sold it to them. I
didn't feel
they would nccd it. They were the ones that asked
for it and it was able to sell very fast.

So while thinking of what you can start doing,
think of people's wants. Humans would be

interested in beauty, health, sex, entertainment, business. So think appropriately.

Find that which they want in these hot areas and sell the hell out of it.

How will you do it?
Use that phone in your hand right now and start something. You don't even need a laptop my dear. So your phone is enough. The laptop can come in later. Make use of what is in your hands champ. Do it now.

Chapter 5

List of online businesses you can do

1. Selling information products:
What are information products? Information products are products where the most important part of what you sell is knowledge.
They are also called digital products because usually, they're sold digitally and can be in the form of courses or tutorials, ebooks, audios, videos, webinars etc.
They are not physical products like bags and shoes that you can feel or touch.

These are the easiest and highest selling products online. This is where I major in and I've taught hundreds of people how to sell them.
If you have any valuable information that can help people in any area of life, you can prepare in form of videos, podcasts, ebooks, webinars and sell it to

them. I'm sure you're thinking now; thinking of what it is you can put together to sell to people. Remember, it must be what people want and will benefit them.
Let me help you figure it out. It can be on business, finance, health, weight loss, fertility, relationship and sex, marriage, beauty, copywriting etc.

Anything around these areas will sell and you don't need to be a writer to write an Ebook that'll sell.
As long as you're able to pass helpful information and teach people one thing or the other in your ebook or course, it'll sell well.

I can teach you how to put it in an ebook format when you figure it out when you're ready. Just send an email to.
annastasiachikodi@gmail.com

2. Affiliate marketing: Affiliate marketing is a business model whereby registered affiliates make a certain amount of commission by selling a product or service created by another person.
In this case, you don't need to worry about the cost of product creation, publication costs, logistics if

any, and all the stress involved in product creation.
All you need to do is to jump on an already established system, register, sell the products to those that need them and make your money.

Affiliate materials can be in the form of services, products or skills.

Examples of companies that use Affiliate marketing models are Amazon (amazon gave this business model a global recognition in the 90's and since then till Affiliate marketing has been on the rising tide generating billions yearly), AliExpress, Jumia, Jimi etc. These companies serve as Affiliate sites.
Affiliate marketing platforms include: clickbank, JVzoo, Herculist, Expertnaire, Learnoflix, digitstem, owo daily to mention but a few.
The business model is very simple. You just have to understand how it works and make money from it.
I've generated millions of naira selling affiliate products and I coach and teach hundreds of people how to generate money online by selling affiliate products. Reach out to me for more information on how to get started.

3. Amazon Kindle Direct Publishing: Do you know that you can write and publish books on Amazon even if you haven't written a book all your life?
I have many people that I have introduced this business to that have published more than 5 books on Amazon. What of my kid brother that's just 17? I got the course for him 2 months ago and he has already published two journals on amazon.

Yes, this is a very simple business model that even enables you to earn in dollars.
All you need to do is to get a course that will teach you step by step on how to go about it and there you go.
When your book or Journal fees are published and people read it or buy, you'll get paid in dollars.
One of my students that published his book two months ago has already made more than 500 dollars from Amazon. People are generating thousands of dollars from this business model.

If you need more information concerning this business model, you can contact me. I'll explain it more to you and teach you how you can get started.

4. Selling recharge cards and data online (VTU business): This business model has made many people rich.

One virtue you need here is consistency.

I know of 3 friends doing amazingly well in this area; **Dr Ifeanyi of @unidata.com.ng, Dr Chinedum of @Dataisoxygen and Dr. Ikpeama of @rhemadata.com.**

Dr. Ifeanyi even calls it the NEW OIL WELL and he has been teaching people how they can start with just a little capital. They have really made a fortune from this business and this is because they know their unions and they run it the right way.

 If you are interested in this, check them out online or you reach out to me so I can connect you to them.

5. Public speaking and public education:

This is another way you can win big online.

Enlightening the entire public and educating them sets you apart for something big you'd never know.

It wouldn't happen overnight but with night, you'll see how all attention would be drawn to you.

You can't go wrong by becoming valuable to people.

The best thing you can do for someone is to let them know what they didn't know.

You do this online consistently for 2 to 3 months and you'll see what will happen.

Do not always focus on engagement; how many people liked and commented on your posts. That will discourage you. Focus on the impression. Focus on your value creation. The money will definitely come with time.

6. Real Estate: Wow! The benefits of this cannot be over -emphasized. This has gone beyond the old way of selling houses.
This is a modern and organized way of making money by selling real estate properties. They are also called realtors.

Steps to take to get started:
1. Get a real estate license
2.Find a brokerage
3. Find a mentor
4. Learn how it works
5. Build your personal brand.
You can read more about this later.

Other things you can do online include:

1. Copywriting
2. Graphic and web designing
3. Ecommerce etc.
4. Non fungible token (NFT) etc.

I can help you with the courses that'll teach you how to go about each and every one of these areas.

Now that you have an idea of what I'm talking about, you can add yours to the list but don't stop there. Start it!

Chapter 6

Start it (Research and Startup)

Every idea remains a dream or plan until it is acted upon.
The goals you've not acted upon remain plans.
How would you know that it'll work if you don't give it a try?
This step is the most critical part in any project.
This is the step that has made plans to remain untouched and goals to remain unmet for years.

Newton's law of motion states that a body remains at rest, or in motion at a constant speed in a straight line, unless acted upon by a force.
This means that nothing will change until you act on it. You cannot start making money online until you start taking the necessary actions that will bring you closer to that goal.

Now, how do you start?
1. Make a proper research about the area and niche you want to go into.

It's just like in marriage. Would you marry someone you don't know?
Even in some cultures, the families involved would travel to their intended inlaws community to make inquiries about each other's families.
The type of family they are, the sicknesses that run in their family, their attitude towards others etc.
This is the same way it is with business.
If you want to have the best in your business, then proper research is very important.
Some of the online businesses would require you buying a course and studying it. This is the stage where you do them.

Now let me talk about start up and start up capital.
This is where most people encounter difficulties.
Anyone that ever wanted to start up any business was once in this dilemma but the difference is in the way it is handled.
Some people found their way out, others tried and got tired while the rest didn't even try raising the money.
I was once here. It's not a good place to be in. But if you figure it out, you will feel like a winner.
First of all, I want you to adopt that Prosperity mindset I discussed in chapter 2.

Money should never limit you from starting your online business.

Ways to raise money for your online business:

1. Start with the little things: You can start by creating ebooks or doing those businesses you can start with little money so you can raise money to start the bigger projects.
You can even host some seminars/training where you charge people a small amount of money to teach them something that'll benefit them.
I know what is going on in your mind. You're probably asking yourself what you know that you can teach others; yes! Think out loud champ! There must be something you're good at. You must be more than 15 years old, meaning that you've gained 15 years of experience on earth.

2. Leverage on good debts: What is a good debt you might ask?
 Good debt is often exemplified in the old adage "it takes money to make money." If the debt you take on helps you generate income and build your net worth, then that can be considered a good one.

Any money that you're borrowing to invest into knowledge or your life is a good debt because you are going to make 10 times of it when the results start coming.
Examples of good debts include money you used to acquire Education, High income skills, real estates, courses, houses.

Good debt has the potential to increase your net worth or enhance your life in an important way.

Now,what is bad debt? Yes! We also have bad debt. Bad debt involves borrowing money to purchase rapidly depreciating assets or only for the purpose of consumption. Bad debt is the money you borrowed to buy hair, to eat, to buy clothing,to buy a phone (unless you've decided to use that phone to generate money), borrowing to clear debt.
Bad debt will make you more broke. Bad debt will make you beg more. It is not increasing your net worth. It is not creating more wealth for you.
It is of no benefit to you. By all means, avoid bad debt.

So if you can borrow to start that business knowing that you'd do your best to make the best out of it, borrow.

I'm giving you this advice because it has worked
for me twice and it profited me. Even my Affiliate
marketing business, I borrowed to start it.
But I didn't borrow it from one person.
I wrote down the names of 10 people and called
them one by one to help me with 10k each. It'll be
easier for someone to loan you 10k than to loan
you 50k or 100k. They can easily forfeit 10k but
they cannot forfeit 50k so they are more likely to
loan you 10k than 50k.
At the end of the day, I was able to raise 50k from
3 persons and today I've made 7 figures from that
business with lots of knowledge. I have become
better but in mind and in pocket.

So this is a good way to start if you have nothing.
Let's make it practical: write down names of 10
people that can not say no to you today (we all
have them). You can even ask for 5k each. Raise
that money and start that business. If you wait till
you get buoyant enough to start it, you'll wait for
months, years or even decades and then get tired.
Start it now by all means.

Chapter 7

Sell it like crazy.

Most people don't even get to this stage.
Once they start it and don't get results in a week or two or even a month, they give up.
Let me tell you something; it's not all businesses that you will have your customers already waiting for you. Yes, I know I told you to sell what people want but some online businesses would require you to have patience. You'd need to master certain skills first before seeing results. So do not quit when the results are not coming yet. You have to show kp consistently. You should bear in mind that your prospects (potential buyers) are not seeing you so you'd have to take them from the level of being strangers to a level where they can trust you.
Before we talk about the KLT factor, I'd like to list steps you'll follow to make your business a successful one.

1. List building: The most guaranteed way to make money online is to build a list first. In fact, I advise you to build your list first before selling to them. You must know that it is a game of numbers. The higher the numbers, the higher the sales. What do I mean by list building?
Your list is the number of contacts you have or the number of people that are subscribed to your mail. They are a group of people interested in what you're are selling

You must have a good number of them and they must be qualified (can afford what you sell).

2. Nurture your list: This is where starters and businesses suck. That you have a good number of contacts in your list doesn't qualify them as customers.
You need to Nurture them. You need to make them believe. You need to make them feel that they are losing out if they don't buy from you. Make them love you and what you sell. Show up daily.
Do it consistently. Do not focus on money, focus on giving them value and making them see the benefit of what you are selling to them. This is where the KLT factor comes in.
K stands for Know. Bear it in mind that 90 percent of your list doesn't know you. So you must help

them to get to know you. What you do, what your daily activity looks like. Help them know that you're real and not a scammer. Most of them must have been victims of circumstances on the online space.

L stands for Like: you have to make them like you.
Post the things that would interest them.
Post the things that are valuable. Educate them.
Make them like you and what you sell.

T stands for Trust: why should they leave their busy schedule and trust you and your business? Why should they trust you to entrust their money in your hands?
Until you bring your prospects to this level, you're yet to succeed and sell crazily in your business. Who knows you likes you and trusts you matters in the world of business.

3. Handle prospect's objections: people are scared of doing things online because they've been scammed severely by online vendors in the past. So until you help them overcome their fears, you wouldn't close that sale. Help your prospect overcome their fears. Help them trust you and what you're selling.

4. Position yourself as an authority: this is the only way people would listen to you. You have to be bold enough while giving value. Your profile picture across social media platforms should be professional.

Make them believe so much in you. Do not ever make them feel that you don't know what you're doing. Be valuable to them.

5. Post valuable contents consistently: Give them reasons to always pause when they see your update and read. Enlighten them. Teach them. You know that it is an online business, so for you to be rich in pocket you need to be well informed. Also bear in mind that most things you'll be dealing with are information and digital products, so help your audience know more everyday about them.

Do it consistently. Do not stop. Focus on impressions, not engagements.

6. Close the sale: Sell to your list crazily once you're done qualifying them.

Maximize every opportunity to sell to them.

Run offers like small discounts, free gifts, free classes, appreciation. Your offers must be mouth watering.

You have to understand that you're dealing with people's emotions because humans are so emotional. Make them feel loved and understood. Treat them like they're special. Be there for them. Don't run away after they've bought from you. They are your asset for life and you should do everything to keep them loyal. You get the point?

7. Discipline: You have to treat your online business as a business and not as a hobby. If you treat it like a hobby, it'll still give you a hobby kind of result.
When you treat it as a business, you'll get the results you desire and deserve.

Show up daily. Maximize the social media platforms.
Post valuable contents on social media platforms. You can use the weekend to prepare the contents you'll use for the week, save them in your note app so you don't run out of contents during the week. Social media platforms you can maximize: Facebook, Instagram, tiktok, LinkedIn, pinterest, Twitter etc.
Make like 10 tweets and one thread daily. Read books, watch motivational videos, and listen to podcasts so you can be full of knowledge.

This is what I do on a daily basis no matter how tired I am.
This doesn't mean you should copy people back to back, just model them. Tweak it to your taste. Write your contents from your own mind and intuition.

I know why I'm saying this because each and every one 9f us is special and we all have our own unique ways of doing things. Even if you have your Done For Yous (DFY), you should still tweak it to your taste and how your audience would love it.
This is what will differentiate you from the rest and help you get your desired results.
Engage in people's posts. Look for groups on Facebook where you'll likely find your target audience. Engage regularly and drop valuable comments on those posts.
Make sure your contents end with a call to action by dropping a link to your website or WhatsApp so your target audience can connect to you.

8. Scale up your business: This is what will make you rich and turn you to a million dollar champ in your business.
Most people don't even get here and that is why you see most entrepreneurs pulling out after some months.

Like I said before, business is a game of numbers
so it goes beyond people you know now.
When you finish selling to those you know and
those referred to you, would you pause your
business?
What would you do? This is why scaling up your
business comes in.
With the money you've made from organic ads and
sales, you can start running your ads on various
social media platforms.
This is what I mean by scaling up your business.

You know those adverts you usually see on your
timeline that have SPONSORED written under
them?
They are being paid for. These are the people that
want to take their businesses to the next level.

This is why you shouldn't squander all your money
when you start making sales. Why you may ask?
Inorganic ads (sponsored or paid ads) is a type of
ads you pay to run. You see? When you kick off
that business and start making sales, you
shouldn't eat the whole money. Keep a greater
portion so you can use it for your sponsored ads
which will make you richer. Here, you're selling to
people you don't know.

But now when they connect with you, use the steps above to convert them from strangers to customers.
Run your ads continuously. Do it daily. Do not stop.

How do you qualify these prospects?
By using a strong sales funnel.
What is a sales funnel? A sales funnel is a series of steps your prospects go through before they'll become customers.
For me; it's Ads - landing page (website) - WhatsApp YouTube -back to WhatsApp.
For some people; it's Ads to WhatsApp. For others, it's Ads to websites to Email.

This means that for you to scale up your business, you should have your landing page, sometimes option page and thank you page. Landing page is a website where you explain what your business is all about. So when anybody sees your ad running and clicks on the link, It will bring the person to the landing page, then to your WhatsApp once they click on the call to action button or to subscribe to your email list or to attend your live webinars.

No business ever succeeds without ads. This is how you win big. So if you're already selling in your business, start running ads right now to 10x your income.

Akin Alabi during one of our summits said "if you can make 10 sales organically in a week, why not triple it by running ads?" This is it! This is how to be rich in pocket. It is a numbers game.
If possible, learn how to run ads so you can run your ads by yourself. It will really go a long way to help you. For example; let's say you major in writing ebooks. You can write many ebooks and upload them on your website or 3rd party websites like Selar and then run ads to these websites continuously.
This is how to make it big online. This is what white people do. They write ebooks almost everyday and upload them in their websites, then run ads daily to those websites. Wait, you still haven't started doing something yet? Wow! You should start thinking out something and do it immediately.

Before I forget; if you want to get a course that'll teach you how to run profitable ads, you can contact me and I'll get the course across to you.

Start running those ads now, even if you're doing
an offline business.
You can run ads on Facebook, Instagram, Twitter
or LinkedIn. Any of these platforms is good.
When those desired results start coming, repeat
the process, create continuous flow of wealth.
That is how to do it.

Chapter 8

Busy Schedule? Time management.

"Time is a created thing.
To say,'I don't have time' is to say, 'I don't want
to." - Lao Tzu.

"If you spend so much time thinking about a
thing, you'll never get it done"....Bruce Lee.

Do you want to know the truth? Time isn't your
problem.
You are not doing something not because of time
but because you just haven't decided to start it.
As a Medical doctor, I've come to the conclusion
that as long as I spend most of my time in the
hospital I can still achieve every other thing I want
to achieve. Stay at home mum, 9 to 5 worker,
pastor, student etc, you can start a side hustle
today.
The excuse I get daily is; Anna I don't have time
for this.
Anna, my work is taking too much of my time.

Ma'am, I'm a Medical student so I can't combine books and business.
I understand your plea. I'm not disputing the fact that your career or field is taking too much from you.
I know and understand this feeling because I'm wearing the same shoe.
In this chapter, I'll just give you ideas that are working for me and others that are doing well both in business and their primary profession.
It starts depending on your life goals and what you want out of life.
If what you're doing now can get you to where you're going in life, fine and good. If you're content with where you are right now, then this isn't for you.
But I'm sure you spent your money to buy this book to read because you want more out of life.
Trust me, you have time if you do proper planning.

Like me, I break down my goals daily, sometimes weekly or monthly and this has helped me.
I'm not saying that I've perfected in this but this is something that should guide you.
First, know what you want.
Write it down.

You know the nature of your work. You know your working hours so you'll do this assignment yourself.

Let me give you an advice my colleague in business gave me;
I was just telling her how my job was taking my time during one of our business meetings. Do you know what she told me? She said; "Anna I understand the nature of your work, how time consuming it is because my sister is a doctor too. But see what you can do....create your contents during the weekends and save them in your notepad.
Prepare them and keep. All you need to do each day is just to copy and paste. I have a doctor friend that is making millions of naira weekly just by selling courses online and I'm sure it's the same thing you're doing. So plan yourself very well".
I have done this for 2 weeks now and I can see a great improvement in my business.

Let me also give you the advice I got from my company's admin. He said, " Anna, outsource. Get your business working and teach people the work so they can be working for you eyen you're not there.

Let them handle replying to your messages, posting on your social media platforms while you focus on closing the sale. Just find these secondary school graduates that are still seeking admission, teach them the work and pay them monthly. It will help you greatly ". That was a great relief to me. These are not just mere suggestions, they are strategies that are working for many. I know of most people in my company that do these and they're closing sales crazily which in turn enriches their pockets.

Like I said before, not what you want.

What are the irrelevant distractions that are taking your damn time? Social media, friends, laziness, procrastination, fear, shiny object syndrome, Netflix? Give up everything that is holding you back my dear. It's not worth it. Unless you don't want to change the trajectory.

You must sacrifice something to get what you want.
It can either be your time, your energy or your resources. You must give up one thing to build the future you want. You must give up distractions to achieve your life goals. Know what to do and when to do them.

The most difficult thing is to start. Once you start,
you'll figure it all out.

We all have 24 hours in a day. You can use it
anyhow you want but you can never regain it.
Maybe you haven't seen or heard; people are into
many things.
Do you think the wealthy people you see today
have only one stream of income? No friend; they
have 2, 3 or even 4. It is called wealth creation. You
create streams of wealth so that one can back up
the other.

Be wise as a serpent and gentle as a dove.
Write that goal now and dedicate your time to each
task to help you achieve them.
Start from the hardest task (biggest frog) and do
the easier ones in between.

You have books to read? Exams to prepare?
Children to take care of? They are all valid reasons
but someone out there is doing all these and is still
doing well in business. It all falls back to what you
want out of life. So stop overthinking it and start
already.

Chapter 9

Life investment and financial intelligence.

Some people didn't learn this early in life and they're paying for it today. I have asked successful people many questions and one thing I learnt from all of them is financial intelligence.
My mentor would always say; make sure you invest into your future. Make sure that you're bringing out a portion of any money you're making now for investment or savings.
I know that saving wouldn't really profit you much but by all means, save.

When that money starts flowing in, make sure you are not spending everything because it is not always going to be like that.
Buy lands, buy shares and stocks, invest in real estate, invest in knowledge so you'll be able to yun your business in a better way, save in dollars so it'll keep appreciating as the dollar price rises. Do

not spend it all no matter the situation you find
yourself in.

I didn't learn this on time but I'm glad I know
better now.
I know of a friend that won a car but he sold it to
buy land. This is financial intelligence. He is
building wealth for the future. Land is something
that appreciates but if he had driven that car, it'll
have lost it's value in two years. I didn't say you
shouldn't drive a car but can you maintain it? Have
you really built enough? Just do what works for
you but no go dey do pass yourself. Invest ! Save!
Spend wisely!

Chapter 10

The place of God in your life and business.

My dear, it all starts with God. I'll be a fool to finish this book without mentioning God.
Wow! It can only be God. He is the one that will open the eyes of your understanding and flood it with light that'll help you excel.
He is the one that will make you wiser than your peers and contemporaries.
Deuteronomy 8 vs 18 says " But remember the LORD your God, for it is He who gives you the ability to produce wealth and so confirms His covenant, which He swore to your ancestors as it is today ".
Every skill and special talent we think we have today is given to us by God.

Without Him, there's no us and there'll be no success story. You might ask me; what of non

Christians that succeed in business but I also need you to understand that we have good success and bad success. It depends on the one you want to have.
But if you must succeed, then you must do it with God.

Proverbs 16 vs 3: "Commit thy works unto the Lord and thy thoughts shall be established ".
When you create that business idea and plan and share it with God, He will never fail you. He will even give you more ideas.

This will start by building a strong relationship with Him if you haven't. His blessings maketh rich and a depth no sorrow and His desire is that we succeed.

Even when you make it in this business you're about to start, do not forget your roots. Your root is God.

One of my mentors and sister won a car some weeks ago from our company. The first thing she did when she came home and saw that car in their compound is to kneel down and worship God. As she was doing that, I broke down in tears. She said, " Lord everything I have today, You're the one that gave me. You knew how it all began and you've been there till now. So thank you Lord". This is her second time winning a car and she has traveled to 4 different countries through this business.

Can't you see how faithful God is? This is why you shouldn't let Him down. Start this business with Him and watch Him prove Himself in your life. How about me? God is the best thing that ever happened to me. In fact, you wouldn't be reading this book by Anna today if God isn't in my story. Make Him part of your story today and watch him prosper you.

Conclusion:

Wow! I've said a lot in this short book that can help anybody that is ready to run.
Now I need you to gather the courage to do this with me. I have prayed for you already even before you bought this book. So you are not just reading a book, you are being opened to a different dimension of greatness. So are you willing to plant this seed of greatness today?
What is your goal?
What is your why? Is your "Why" big enough?
What is your obsession?
What is your addiction?
Can the answer be **SUCCESS**?
Do you know you have what it takes to do anything?
Do you know that the world is waiting for you?

I wish you the very best champ! Go in this might and succeed! As you've enriched your mind with this book, go now and enrich your pocket. I will see you at the top. Remember, "you can't fly with the eagles if you continue to scratch with the turkeys".
---- *Zig Ziglar.*
May the grace of God be with you.

Connect with me on my social media handles for more valuable information .

LinkedIn
https://www.linkedin.com/in/annastasia-nze-chi kodi-342426189

Twitter
https://twitter.com/.NzeAnnastasia

Instagram
https://instagram.com/the_annastasiachika?igsh id=YmMyMTA2M2Y=

Facebook
https://www.facebook.com/annastasia.chika.5

Send in your reviews about this book on the email below
annastasiachikodi@gmail.com.

Do not skip this. It will help me know your thoughts .
Your friend, Annastasia